PROTECT OR PERISH: *The Complete Guide to Patent Strategy, Global Protection, and Avoiding Costly Mistakes*

By: Ruben Alcoba, Esq.

COPYRIGHT PAGE

Published by Alcoba Law Group, P.A. Miami, Florida www.miamipatents.com

First Edition: April 2026

ISBN: [To be assigned] Library of Congress Control Number: [To be assigned]

Disclaimer This book is for general informational and educational purposes only. It does not constitute legal advice and does not create an attorney-client relationship. Patent and intellectual property law are complex and fact specific. Always consult a registered patent attorney licensed in your area before taking any action regarding your invention or intellectual property. Laws, USPTO procedures, and fees change frequently: verify current requirements on official government websites.

Contents

INTRODUCTION

I authored this book for one reason: I have sat across the table from too many inventors and business owners who lost everything, not because their idea was not good, but because no one ever explained the real rules in plain English before it was too late.

I have watched brilliant creators pour years of their lives and life savings into an invention, only to see it copied, blocked, undervalued, or stolen because of a single missed deadline, a weak claim, an unprotected disclosure, or a "too-good-to-be-true" deal with the wrong people. Each time it happens, it hurts the same way. The inventor does not just lose money, they lose confidence, momentum, and sometimes the dream that kept them going through late nights and long odds.

That pain is what drives me.

As a registered patent attorney who has personally handled thousands of patent and trademark matters, I have spent more than 25 years on the front lines helping inventors and entrepreneurs protect what they build. I have seen the hope in their eyes when they walk in with a prototype and the quiet devastation when they return months later because something preventable went wrong. This book is my attempt to change that pattern.

I wrote it with empathy, not lectures. Every chapter draws inspiration from real conversations I have had with clients: people who are intelligent, hardworking, and enthusiastic, though unfamiliar with the patent system until they needed to learn about the system. My goal is simple: to give you the straight talk, the practical strategies, and the hard-won lessons so you can protect your invention, your time, and your future before the mistakes happen.

If you are holding this book, you are already ahead of most inventors. You are choosing education over assumption. You are deciding that your idea deserves more than hope, it deserves a real strategy.

I wrote this for you.

Ruben Alcoba, Esq.

Registered Patent Attorney

Alcoba Law Group, P.A.

THE PROTECT OR PERISH FRAMEWORK

Every inventor who succeeds, and everyone who loses everything, passes through the same five critical points.

I call this the Protect or Perish Framework™.

1. EXPOSURE (The Danger Zone)

The moment your idea leaves your head, you are at risk.

- Talking to partners
- Showing prototypes
- Posting online

Mistake: Exposure without protection
Solution: File before you speak

2. FOUNDATION (The Filing Strategy)

What you file, and how you file, determines everything.

- Weak filings = weak protection
- Wrong filings = no protection

Mistake: Filing cheap or incomplete
Solution: Strategic, layered filings

3. CONTROL (Market Positioning)

Patents are not just protection. They are leverage.

Mistake: Filing and doing nothing
Solution: Use IP to control competitors

4. DEFENSE (Enforcement & Risk)

If you cannot enforce it, you do not own it.

Mistake: Ignoring infringement
Solution: Strategic enforcement posture

5. MONETIZATION (Turning IP into Money)

The end goal is not a patent.
The end goal is value.

Licensing
Valuation
Exit leverage

Most inventors fail in one of these five areas. This book exists to make sure you don't.

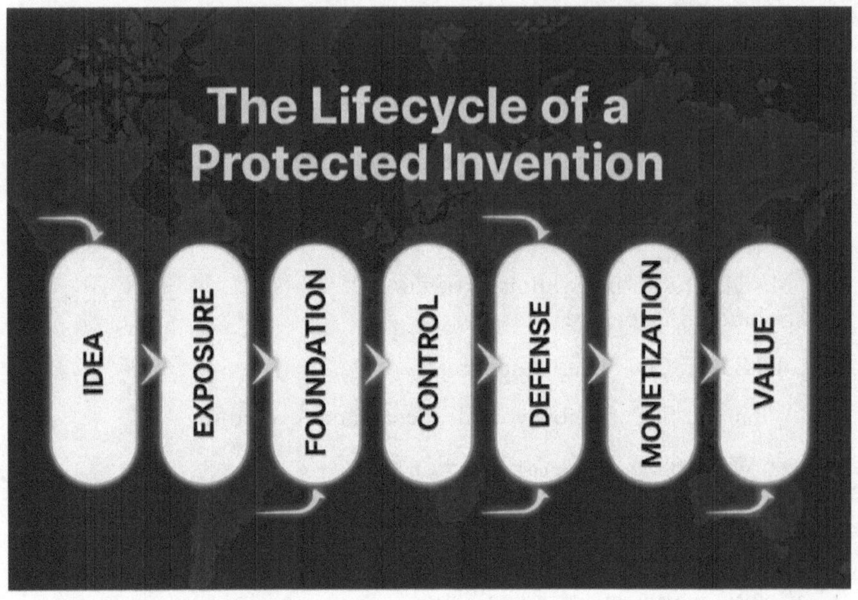

PART I – FOUNDATIONS OF PATENT PROTECTION

Part I: Foundations of Patent Protection

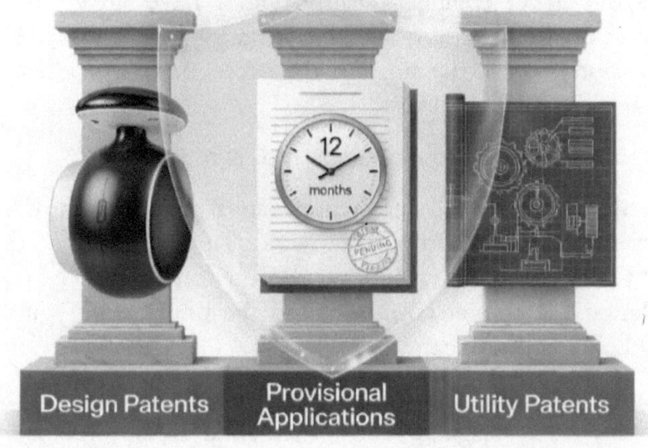

Chapter 1: What Is a Design Patent? How to Protect the Look of Your Product (and What It Actually Costs to File)

People do not fall in love with how your product works first. They fall in love with how it *looks*.

Before a customer ever reads the specs, clicks "add to cart," or understands the clever engineering inside, they have already made a snap decision based on shape, color, and that instant "I want that" feeling. That visual impression is often the single biggest reason your product stands out or gets lost in a sea of look-alikes.

A design patent is the tool that lets you own that look.

Most inventors pour all their energy into protecting how something *works* (utility patents) and completely overlook the appearance that sells it. The result? Competitors copy the exact aesthetic that makes your product recognizable, customers get confused, and the brand edge you worked so hard to build quietly disappears.

A design patent changes that equation. Under U.S. law (35 U.S.C. § 171) it protects any new, original, and ornamental design for an article of manufacture. In plain English: if someone copies the way your product looks, you can legally stop them.

Unlike a utility patent, a design patent has only one claim: "The ornamental design as shown." That single sentence makes your drawings the entire scope of your rights. What you show is what you protect: nothing more, nothing less. Shape, configuration, surface ornamentation, and overall aesthetic are all fair game. Function, mechanics, and how it performs inside? Not covered at all. If the design is purely functional, it will not qualify.

The protection lasts 15 years from the date the patent is granted. During that window you control who can make, use, or sell products that look like yours. You can license the design, use it in negotiations, or enforce it when copycats appear.

The tradeoff most inventors miss is this: you only protect what you show in the drawings. File one narrow set of views and a clever competitor can change a few lines or proportions and legally walk right past your patent. That is why strategic filing, multiple related designs, alternative embodiments, and drawings that spotlight the features that make your product instantly recognizable, are so important.

Now let us talk numbers, because every inventor asks the same question: "How much does this actually cost?"

Current USPTO fees (as of early 2026) are as follows:

Fee Type	Micro Entity	Small Entity	Standard Entity
Filing Fee	$44	$88	$220
Search Fee	$32	$64	$160
Examination Fee	$128	$256	$640
Issue Fee	$148	$296	$740
Total USPTO Fees	**$352**	**$704**	**$1,760**

Add professional drawings (required to be USPTO-compliant) at $100–$800 and attorney drafting/strategy fees of $1,000–$3,500. Most inventors who qualify as micro or small entities end up investing a total of $1,500–$5,000 for a properly prepared design patent. That sounds like real money, until you compare it to the cost of watching your visual brand get copied and your market share evaporates.

Many first-time inventors qualify for the lower micro-entity or small-entity rates, so the government portion drops dramatically. The real mistake is trying to save a few hundred dollars on drawings or skipping professional help. Weak drawings equal a weak patent. You are not just filing paperwork; you are creating the legal weapon that will decide whether a copycat must stop or can keep selling.

A colleague at another patent firm told me about an inventor named Mike who launched a sleek, minimalist wireless earbud charging case that doubled as a desktop stand. The curved matte-black housing and signature magnetic alignment groove were what customers raved about in reviews. He had filed a utility patent on the internal charging circuit but never thought about protecting the appearance. Six months later a competitor's version appeared online: same curve, same groove, same matte finish, just a slightly different logo. Mike's sales flattened overnight.

He reached out in frustration. When they analyzed the situation, it became clear that the exact visual features customers loved most were completely unprotected. The competitor was free to copy the look that made his product stand out. Mike watched significant market share evaporate and felt the brand edge he had worked so hard to build quietly disappear. The mistake cost him months of stalled growth and nearly undermined the entire product line.

Instead of rushing into litigation, the firm prepared three targeted design patent applications: one for the primary embodiment, one for an alternative color/finish variation, and one highlighting the magnetic groove detail with broken lines to focus the claim. The drawings were crisp, strategic, and filed within weeks. Once the new patents issued and the competitor received professional notice, they redesigned their product with a distinctly different housing. Mike's sales eventually recovered, but the experience taught him a hard lesson about the real cost of leaving the visual brand unprotected.

The lesson I want you to remember is simple: if the look is what makes your product stand out, protect the look before the market notices. Do not wait until the copycat is already on the shelf. File early, file strategically, and treat the drawings as the most important part of the application. That single mindset shift turns a nice-looking product into a protected business asset.

Should You File a Design Patent?

- Does the look drive customer decisions?
- Would a competitor benefit from copying appearance?
- Is branding tied to the visual design?

If YES → Protect the design early

Key Takeaways You Can Use Today

- A design patent protects only the ornamental appearance shown in the drawings—shape, configuration, and overall look.
- It does *not* protect function, mechanics, or how the product works.
- You get one claim: "The ornamental design as shown." Your drawings *are* your patent.
- Total realistic cost: $1,500–$5,000 (most inventors pay far less thanks to micro/small entity discounts).
- File multiple variations and use strategic drawings, otherwise competitors can design around you easily.
- If the look is what sells your product, protect the look early. Waiting is the most expensive mistake you can make.

Chapter 2: Design Patent Infringement – How Close Is Too Close? (And why the "20% Rule" Is a Dangerous Myth)

If someone copies your product, how do you know it's illegal?

Every inventor and business owner eventually stares at a competitor's new release and asks exactly that question. The product looks close, not identical, but familiar enough that your stomach tightens. And in that moment, the same comforting thought almost always surfaces: "They changed enough of it. They're safe."

Then comes the myth that refuses to die: "As long as they tweak it by 20 percent… or 30 percent… or whatever the latest number floating around online is… it's not infringement."

Let me be blunt: that rule does not exist. It never has. Not in the law, not in any court decision, not in reality. Believing it can quietly destroy years of work and the market edge you fought to earn.

Misunderstanding this single point is expensive. You might not protect what's yours. You might launch a product that unknowingly steps on someone else's toes. Or you might watch your own design get copied while you sit on the sidelines thinking, "They only changed 20 percent, they're fine." None of those outcomes feel good when the invoices start arriving.

So, let's cut through the noise and talk about what design patents protect, and how courts really decide infringement.

A design patent covers only one thing: the ornamental appearance of your product. Not how it works. Not the clever mechanism inside. Just what someone sees when they look at it. That's why the legal test is visual, not technical.

The rule that still governs today comes from a case decided in 1871, *Gorham Co. v. White.* It's simple and surprisingly human: Would an ordinary observer, looking at the two designs side by side, be deceived into thinking they are the same?

That's it. No calculator. No percentage. Just overall visual impression.

This is exactly why the "20 percent rule" is so dangerous. It promises the certainty we all crave, "Change this much and you're golden", but design-patent law refuses to play by math. Visual perception doesn't reduce to numbers. Courts don't count differences; they ask whether the total look fools the eye.

A colleague at another patent firm told me about an inventor named Alex who developed a sleek, award-winning portable charging stand for phones and tablets. He had poured eighteen months and his savings into perfecting the curved base and the signature "floating" cradle that let the device tilt right. Sales were climbing. Then one morning he opened an industry newsletter and saw a nearly identical stand from a competitor: same graceful curve, same floating cradle, just a slightly different color and a couple of small ridges added along the edges.

Alex measured the changes and was certain he was safe. "They changed about 25 percent of the visible surfaces," he told the attorney. "I read online that anything over 20 percent is okay." He was ready to shrug it off and keep building.

The competitor's product stayed on the market. Alex watched his sales suffer as customers struggled to tell the two stands apart. The experience cost him valuable momentum, eroded the market edge he had worked so hard to earn, and brought him dangerously close to watching his biggest visual differentiator get copied for free. It also left him questioning whether design protection was even worth the effort.

When the firm reviewed the two designs side-by-side using the ordinary-observer test, Alex quickly saw what the law sees: the overall visual impression was still too similar. The minor ridges and color swap didn't break the spell. The firm helped him file three additional design patents covering key variations (different angles, alternative cradle positions, and a version with integrated cable routing). The competitor later redesigned with a truly distinct look, but the damage had already been done: months of lost sales and the painful realization that believing the "20% rule" myth had nearly sunk his product line.

That mindset shift, moving from "How much did they change?" to "Does it still look like mine to a regular customer?", is exactly what I want you to take from this chapter.

Key Takeaways You Can Use Today

- There is no 20 percent (or any percent) rule, ever.
- Infringement turns on overall visual impression, not the number of differences.
- Minor changes in color, material, or minor details almost never save you.
- File multiple design patents covering variations, not just one version.

- Before you launch or copy, compare side-by-side through the eyes of a regular customer, not through a ruler or calculator.
- When in doubt, talk to someone who lives and breathes the ordinary-observer test, before the market decides for you.

Chapter 3: Can You File a Provisional Patent for a Design? The Truth That Could Save Your Idea (And Your Money)

If someone offered you a fast, cheap way to get "patent pending" status on your product's look, would you jump on it?

Most inventors say yes without thinking twice. It sounds perfect: lower cost, less paperwork, and that comforting "patent pending" label you can slap on your packaging while you test the market.

Here is the truth almost nobody tells you until it is too late: You cannot file a provisional patent application for a design patent. Not ever. Not with the "right" service. Not in any special circumstance. United States law prohibits this, and the USPTO does not permit it.

Still, every week I encounter inventors who have been misled by flashy online services, so-called "patent coaches," or posts on discussion forums. They spend significant amounts of money but receive absolutely no protection in return.

This single misunderstanding can cost you your filing date, your rights, and sometimes your entire market advantage. And it happens because provisional applications *do* exist… but only for utility patents (the ones that protect how something works). Design patents, the ones that protect how something *looks*, play by completely different rules.

A design patent covers shape, configuration, surface ornamentation, and overall visual appearance. Design patents are regulated by 35 U.S.C. §§ 171–173 and require a fully detailed application from the start, including accurate drawings, a written specification, and a single claim: "The ornamental design as shown." There is no "placeholder" version. No informal filing. You either do it right the first time or you do not get protection.

The myth of the "provisional design patent" creates a dangerous illusion. You think you have locked in a priority date and bought yourself time. In reality, you've filed a document that has no legal effect on your design. When a copycat shows up, you discover you have nothing to enforce.

A colleague at another patent firm told me about a bootstrapping founder named Jordan who designed a striking, ergonomic travel pillow that folded flat in a way no one had seen before. The unique contour and zippered pocket details were what made customers stop scrolling and buy. Looking to save money and move fast, he saw an ad promising "Provisional Design

Patent – Only $399 – Get Patent Pending Today!" and clicked. The service filed the paperwork, sent him a nice-looking certificate, and Jordan started selling with "Patent Pending" proudly printed on every tag.

Sales took off. Then, three months later, a competitor launched an almost identical pillow at a lower price. When Jordan tried to enforce his rights, he discovered the devastating truth: the provisional filing was completely worthless for a design patent. It had never established any priority date and gave him zero legal protection. The competitor stayed on the market, Jordan's sales were undercut, and he watched the exact features that made his product special get copied for free.

By the time he reached out to the other firm he was angry, embarrassed, and worried it was too late. The firm reviewed every photo and drawing, then filed three proper non-provisional design patent applications the same week, covering the primary embodiment, the folded configuration, and the key pocket detail with strategic broken lines. Because he had not publicly disclosed the design more than six months earlier, they were still able to secure solid U.S. filing dates. The competitor, seeing the new patents issue and receiving professional notice, redesigned their product to avoid infringement.

Jordan's sales eventually recovered, but the experience cost him months of lost revenue, damaged momentum, and nearly killed his entire product line before he could fix it. He later called it the most expensive lesson of his career: he had bet his whole business on a shortcut that didn't exist.

Jordan's story is the reason I want you to pause before you click "buy" on any provisional design filing offer. There are no workarounds. The correct path is straightforward:

1. File a full non-provisional design patent application right away.

2. Make sure the drawings are professional and USPTO compliant, every line counts.

3. If you plan to sell internationally, remember the clock is tighter: you have only six months (not twelve) to file abroad and claim priority from your U.S. filing. Miss that window and you can lose rights in foreign markets entirely.

Design patents live and die by precision, not by placeholders. That is why serious inventors treat the first filing as the only filing that matters.

Key Takeaways You Can Use Today

- You cannot file a provisional application for a design patent: period. It provides zero protection and no priority date.

- Design patents require a complete, formal application from day one: drawings are everything.

- File early, before any public disclosure, and treat the first filing as the one that counts.

- If you go international, remember the six-month priority window (not twelve).

- If someone offers you a "provisional design patent," walk away. It is either a misunderstanding or a waste of money.

- Protect the look that makes your product sell by filing correctly the first time. There are no shortcuts, but the right path is simpler and far more powerful than the myth.

Chapter 4: The Power of a Provisional Patent Application – How to Protect Your Idea Before It is Too Late

You are sitting at your desk, it is late at night, you have been thinking about this for weeks, and suddenly the idea hits you. A product. A solution. Something you know could change your business or even your life.

The excitement is real. But right behind it comes the fear: *What if someone else sees it first? What if I talk about it and lose the chance to own it?*

That single moment is exactly why a provisional patent application exists. It is one of the smartest, most powerful first moves an inventor can make if you use it correctly.

In plain English, a provisional patent application is a formal filing with the USPTO under 35 U.S.C. § 111(b) that lets you lock in an early filing date, establish yourself as the first to file, and immediately start using the words "Patent Pending" on your prototypes, website, pitch deck, and packaging. No formal claims. No oath. No USPTO examination. Just a solid description and drawings that fully explain the invention.

It is not a patent. It is a strategic placeholder that buys you up to twelve months of breathing room while you refined the idea, evaluate the market, talked to investors, or decided whether it is worth the full non-provisional filing. But here is the part most people miss, it only works if you treat it like the serious legal document, it is.

The real power is the priority date. The day you file, the USPTO stamps your idea with a permanent timestamp. In America's first-to-file system, that date can mean the difference between owning the invention and watching someone else file a week later and walk away with the rights.

"Patent Pending" is more than marketing fluff. It signals seriousness to investors, deters copycats, and gives you the confidence to share the idea without handing it away for free.

The catch, and it is a big one, is the twelve-month rule. You must file a non-provisional patent application within exactly twelve months or the provisional dies forever. No extensions. No revival. And every detail you hope to claim later must be fully supported in that original provisional. You cannot add new matter when you convert.

Costs are deliberately low to encourage early filing. Current USPTO fees (as of early 2026) are $70 for a micro entity, $140 for a small entity, and $280 for a standard entity. Professional drafting (the part that protects you) typically runs $1,500–$6,000 depending on complexity, but a weak or incomplete provisional is often worse than none at all because it creates false security.

A colleague at another patent firm shared the success story of an inventor named Elena who had designed a clever, space-saving collapsible coffee maker that folded flat for travel or small apartments. The mechanism was elegant, the market was obvious, and she was ready to show it at an upcoming trade show. But she also knew that once she put prototypes in front of strangers, the idea could spread fast.

Instead of rushing ahead unprotected, she reached out to the firm. They filed a strong provisional the same week: detailed description, multiple views of the folding mechanism, and enough technical support to cover every feature she might claim later. She walked into that trade show with "Patent Pending" printed on every prototype and business card.

The reaction was electric. Distributors asked for meetings. An investor who had passed on similar products earlier suddenly wanted in because the IP was already secured. Over the next ten months Elena used the breathing room to perfect the design, run focus groups, and negotiate a small licensing deal. On month eleven they converted the provisional into a full non-provisional application with everything cleanly supported. The patent later issued, the licensing deal closed, and Elena's product is now in stores across three countries.

Elena still tells people the provisional did not just protect her idea; it gave her the confidence to move faster and smarter than she ever could have without it.

Elena's story is the reason I want you to see a provisional not as paperwork, but as a shield, a signal, and a strategy all in one. File early when the invention can be described (not when it is "perfect"). Treat the disclosure requirements seriously. Calendar the twelve-month deadline the day you file. And never treat it like a rough draft you can fix later.

When you do those things, you stop worrying about "What if someone steals this?" and start focusing on "How fast can we bring this to market?"

Should You File a Provisional Patent?

- Can you clearly describe how it works?
- Do you need time to test or raise money?
- Are you about to disclose the idea publicly?

If YES → File immediately
If NO → Refine before filing

Key Takeaways You Can Use Today

- A provisional patent application secures an early filing date and lets you use "Patent Pending" immediately, no claims or examination required.

- It buys you exactly twelve months to refine, test, raise money, or decide on the full patent.

- The disclosure must be complete enough to support everything you want to claim later; you cannot add new matter when converting.

- Costs are low (USPTO fees ~$70–$280 + attorney drafting), but a sloppy provisional creates dangerous false security.

- File when the idea can be described, not when it is perfect, then calendar the twelve-month deadline and plan your next step early.

- Used correctly, it becomes the foundation that turns a good idea into a protected, marketable product.

Chapter 5: How Much Does a Utility Patent Really Cost? The Truth Most Inventors Learn Too Late

The question every inventor asks first is always the same: "How much does a patent cost?"

It sounds simple. But it is the wrong question.

What you are really asking is: "How much do I need to invest so I actually own and protect my idea instead of watching someone else copy it for free?"

A utility patent is not a line item on a spreadsheet. It is a business asset that can block competitors, open licensing deals, raise your company valuation, and give you pricing power for years. And like any serious asset, its price tag has layers, some visible, some hidden, that most inventors only discover after they have already spent the money.

Let us break it down honestly so you can make the decision with your eyes wide open, not after the fact.

The USPTO government fees are the smallest piece of the puzzle. For a non-provisional utility patent application, they currently run roughly:

Current USPTO fees (as of early 2026) are as follows:

- Micro entity: Filing $75 + Search $165 + Examination $190 + Issue $250 = about $680 total
- Small entity: double that
- Large entity: double again

These numbers are deliberately low because the system wants early filings. Real money, and the real value, lives in the professional work that turns your idea into enforceable claims.

Attorney drafting and strategy for a solid non-provisional typically runs $8,000–$15,000. That is not "paperwork." It is the claim drafting, prior-art analysis, technical description, and forward-looking enforcement positioning that determine whether your patent will stop copycats or become a fancy wall decoration.

Then come the hidden costs most inventors never budget for:

- Responding to Office Actions (almost every application gets them): $1,000–$5,000 per response.
- Professional drawings: $300–$600.

- Optional accelerators like Track One expedited examination: $1,050–$4,200.

- Maintenance fees to keep the patent alive after it issues (3.5, 7.5, and 11.5 years): $500–$7,400 each time, depending on your entity size.

Add it all up and the realistic total investment through issuance lands between $10,000–$15,000 for a micro-entity inventor on a straightforward invention and $20,000–$40,000+ for more complex cases or larger entities. That number often shocks people, until they compare it to the cost of losing the market entirely.

The biggest mistake I see is trying to save money on the front end. A cheap online "patent service" or DIY filing almost always produces weak claims that are easy to design around. You end up with a patent that looks impressive on paper but gives you zero real protection when it matters.

A colleague at another patent firm told me about an inventor named Marcus who invented a compact, modular sensor system that let small manufacturers monitor machine health in real time. He was bootstrapping and saw an ad promising a "complete utility patent for only $2,997." He jumped on it to save money. Six months later the application was filed, but the claims were so narrow and poorly written that any halfway-clever competitor could work around them.

When a major industrial supplier expressed serious interest in licensing, their in-house counsel took one look at the patent and walked away. Marcus lost what could have been a seven-figure deal overnight. He watched his competitive edge evaporate, investors pulled back, and he realized too late that he had gambled his entire market position on a low-cost filing that gave him almost no real protection.

The firm showed him side-by-side what a properly drafted set of claims looked like versus what he had. They then filed a new continuation application with strong, strategically written claims, professional drawings, and a full prior-art strategy. The investment was significantly higher than the original $2,997, but it was the right one. Within nine months the strengthened patent issued, the supplier came back to the table, and Marcus closed a licensing deal that more than paid for the entire process.

Marcus's story is the reason I want you to flip the question from "How cheap can I do this?" to "What is my invention worth if it's properly protected?" Because a strong utility patent can block competitors, command royalties, and make your business far more attractive to investors or acquirers. The difference between a weak patent and a bulletproof one is never the government fees, it is the quality of the drafting and the strategy behind it.

Key Takeaways You Can Use Today

- A utility patent is a multi-year investment, not a one-time filing, budget for drafting ($8k–$15k), prosecution responses, drawings, and maintenance fees.
- Government fees are minimal; most costs come from expert claim drafting and strategy.
- Cheap filings always produce weak, easily designed-around patents, do not gamble your market edge to save money upfront.
- A weak patent is permission for competitors.
- Plan for the full lifecycle: expect $10k–$40k+ total through issuance depending on complexity and entity size.
- Focus on value, not price: a strong patent creates exclusivity, licensing revenue, and higher business valuation.
- If your invention has real commercial potential, treat the patent as a business weapon, build it right the first time.

Chapter 6: What Is a Utility Patent Application? The One Filing That Determines Whether You Truly Own Your Invention

You do not own your invention the day the idea hits you. You do not own it when you build the prototype. You do not even own it after you file a provisional patent application.

The only moment true ownership begins is the day you file a properly drafted utility non-provisional patent application with the USPTO.

That single filing is what turns your idea into a legal monopoly: enforceable rights that can block competitors, attract investors, and generate licensing revenue for up to twenty years. Do it right and you control the invention. Do it wrong and you may end up with nothing more than an expensive piece of paper and a painful lesson.

A utility non-provisional patent application is the formal document filed under 35 U.S.C. § 111(a) that asks the USPTO to examine your invention and, if it qualifies, grant you a patent. It covers processes, machines, manufactures, or compositions of matter, anything functional that solves a real problem. Unlike a provisional application, this is the real game: it requires claims, gets substantively examined, and can become an issued patent with teeth.

Most inventors think "I already filed a provisional, so I'm good." That is the trap. A provisional is just a placeholder; it buys you twelve months and "patent pending" status but gives you zero enforceable rights. The non-provisional is where ownership is decided.

Here is what must be in that application because every piece has legal consequences:

- **The Specification**: A complete, clear written description that teaches someone skilled in your field exactly how to make and use the invention (35 U.S.C. § 112). You must also disclose the best mode you know. Skimp here and your patent can be rejected or later invalidated.

- **The Claims**: These are the heart of your patent. They are not a summary; they are the legal boundaries of what you own. Every word matters. Strong claims give you broad protection; weak or narrow ones let competitors design around you easily.

- **Drawings**: Required when they help explain the invention. They support the claims and often make the difference in examination.

- **Oath or Declaration**: You swear you are the true inventor.
- **Information Disclosure Statement (IDS)**: You must tell the USPTO about all known prior art. Hide something and risk the entire patent becoming unenforceable.

Once filed, the USPTO examines novelty, non-obviousness, utility, and proper description. Most applications receive rejections (Office Actions), and you respond with amendments or arguments. The entire process typically takes 18–36 months, sometimes longer in crowded fields.

"Patent pending" is just a warning label. Only an issued patent is a weapon.

The biggest mistake inventors make is treating the non-provisional like a formality they can dash off quickly or handle with templates. You cannot fix everything later. Your priority date is locked in, new matter cannot be added, and weak claims today become easy design-arounds tomorrow.

A colleague at another patent firm told me about an inventor named Chris who had invented a lightweight, tool-free mounting system for rooftop solar panels that cut installation time by 60 percent. He filed a provisional on his own, then six months later used an online template service to file the non-provisional for under $2,000. He figured he was saving money and moving fast. The application was filed, but the claims were vague and narrow, the description skipped key details on how the quick-lock mechanism worked, and he forgot to cite a key piece of prior art he had seen.

Eight months later a competitor launched an almost identical system. Chris tried to send a cease-and-desist letter using the "patent pending" status, but the competitor's attorney immediately pointed out the weaknesses in the filing. The claims would not hold up, the missing disclosure created invalidity risks, and Chris had almost no real leverage. Sales stalled, investors pulled back, and he was staring at the very real possibility of losing the market he had created.

The firm reviewed the filing, showed him exactly where it fell short, and filed a new continuation application the same week. They rewrote the specification with full enablement, drafted broad yet defensible claims around the unique locking geometry, added professional drawings, and properly disclosed all prior art. Because the original filing date was still alive, they kept his priority. Within fourteen months the strengthened patent issued. The competitor, seeing the new claims, redesigned and approached Chris for a licensing discussion instead of a fight. Chris not only kept his market, but he also turned the threat into royalty income.

Chris later said the experience changed how he thinks about every filing. That mindset shift, treating the non-provisional as the most important business document you will ever sign, is exactly what I want you to take away.

The filing is not the win. Control is the win.

Key Takeaways You Can Use Today

- A utility non-provisional patent application is the only filing that can become an enforceable patent, provisional filings are just placeholders.
- Claims are everything: they define exactly what you own and what you can enforce.
- The specification must fully enable and describe the invention; incomplete disclosure cannot be fixed later.
- Expect Office Actions and plan for responses, examination is where most applications are won or lost.
- File correctly the first time: weak or rushed non-provisionals create permanent weaknesses that competitors will exploit.
- If your invention has real commercial value, treat the non-provisional as the most important business document you will ever sign, get professional strategy behind it.

PART II - GLOBAL STRATEGY AND RISK MANAGEMENT

Chapter 7: How a U.S. Provisional Patent Can Destroy Your International Rights (If You're Not Careful)

What if the very first step you take to protect your invention quietly wipes out your chance to protect it in Europe, China, Japan, or any other major market?

It sounds dramatic. It is not.

Every month I watch inventors file a U.S. provisional patent application feeling smart and safe, only to discover later that their own actions (or inactions) have permanently closed the door on international patents. Not because they broke a rule on purpose, but because they never knew the rule existed.

A provisional application is a powerful tool. It gives you a low-cost way to lock in an early filing date, buy yourself up to twelve months to refine the invention, raise money, or evaluate the market, and slap "patent pending" on your product. But it is not protection. It is a ticking clock, and if you miss a single beat, the clock wins.

The Paris Convention gives you exactly twelve months from the provisional filing date to file a U.S. non-provisional, a PCT international application, or direct foreign applications while keeping your original priority date. Do it right and the entire world treats your invention as if you filed everywhere on Day 1. Miss it, or disclose the invention publicly before you file abroad, and in most foreign countries your own provisional (and everything you did afterward) becomes prior art that blocks your patent forever.

Europe is the harshest example. Under the European Patent Convention, novelty is absolute. One public disclosure, your website, a trade-show demo, an investor pitch, even a Kickstarter page, and the invention is no longer "new." No grace period. No "we didn't mean to." Game over.

The second trap is equally common: filing a thin or incomplete provisional. You sketch the basic idea, file quickly, then spend the next year improving it. When you finally file the PCT, the foreign examiner looks back at that original provisional and says, "Sorry, these new details aren't supported by what you filed twelve months ago." Your priority claim is rejected. Suddenly you are fighting the same prior art you thought you had escaped.

A colleague at another patent firm told me about an inventor named Tyler who developed a compact, foldable drone controller that used a unique magnetic hinge system. The concept was strong, the market was ready, and he was bootstrapping. He filed a provisional application himself for under $300, celebrated the "patent pending" status, and immediately started showing prototypes to potential distributors and posting teaser videos online. He figured he had a full year before he needed to worry about the rest of the world.

Sales momentum built fast. At month ten he finally sat down to file the PCT. That is when the international attorney he hired delivered the bad news: his early videos and distributor emails counted as public disclosures. Europe, Japan, and other key markets were now permanently closed. The provisional itself was also too high-level to support the detailed hinge claims he wanted. Tyler watched the cost of international protection skyrocket and entire territories slip away forever.

He reached out to the other firm in a panic. They could not resurrect the lost foreign rights, but they strengthened the U.S. side and helped him pivot. The experience cost him six-figure international opportunities and forced him to redesign and refocus his entire business on the North American market while he still had options. Tyler later called it one of the most painful and expensive lessons of his career: a single provisional filed without a global plan had quietly destroyed the very markets that could have made his product a global success.

Tyler's story is the reason I want you to treat every provisional filing like the start of a global strategy, not the end of one. Here is the practical playbook that protects you:

1. File a strong provisional: full technical description, detailed drawings, enough support to cover every feature you might claim later. Think of it as a real patent application minus the formal claims.

2. Control every public disclosure. NDAs for investors, confidential prototypes, no website launches or social posts until you are ready to file abroad.

3. Calendar the twelve-month deadline the day you file, and start working on the next step at least three months early.

4. Decide early whether the invention has real international potential. If yes, budget for the PCT or foreign filings and plan them as carefully as the first provisional.

Done correctly, a provisional gives you breathing room and a powerful early date. Done carelessly, it becomes the reason you lose the very markets that could have made your product a global success.

Key Takeaways You Can Use Today

- A provisional patent application is a twelve-month clock, not protection.
- Miss the deadline or disclose publicly too early and you can permanently lose patent rights in Europe and most other countries.
- File a complete, detailed provisional that fully supports every future claim.
- Control disclosures with NDAs and confidentiality until you file internationally.
- Plan your global strategy on Day 1, do not treat the provisional as a "set it and forget it" move.
- If your invention has international upside, the provisional is only the first step. Treat every step after it with the same seriousness.

Chapter 8: The Hidden Dangers of International Patents – How Inventors Lose Their Rights in Europe and Asia (And Do not Even Know It)

Most inventors do not lose their patent rights because a clever competitor outsmarted them. They lose them because of a quiet mistake they never saw coming.

And the most expensive mistakes always happen when they try to take their invention overseas: to Europe, China, Japan, Korea, or anywhere else that matters. The rules are not just different from the U.S.; they are unforgiving. One missed deadline, one early disclosure, or one weak sentence in the original filing can permanently shut the door on entire continents.

This chapter is not meant to scare you. It is meant to arm you. Because once you understand the traps, you can avoid them and build the global protection your invention deserves.

The biggest trap is the 30/31-month deadline. When you file a PCT (international) application, you have exactly 30 or 31 months from your earliest priority date to "enter" each country you care about. Miss that window even by one day and you lose the right to file there, forever. No extensions, no "we'll fix it later." The clock is absolute.

The second trap is absolute novelty. In the United States you get a one-year grace period after public disclosure. In Europe and most of Asia there is none. Any public disclosure, your website, a trade-show demo, an investor pitch, a Kickstarter page, even a casual LinkedIn post, before you file can destroy your patent rights in those countries permanently.

Then come the drafting dangers. Europe prohibits "added subject matter." If your original application does not already contain enough detail to support every claim you later want, you cannot add it. The claims get narrowed or rejected. Translation errors in China, Japan, or Korea can quietly shrink your protection without you realizing it until enforcement time. And if your application covers more than one invention, the search authority may force you to split it and pay extra fees or leave entire features unprotected.

These mistakes do not announce themselves. You feel safe because you filed in the U.S. Then one day you try to expand and discover the doors are locked to expansion.

A colleague at another patent firm told me about an inventor named Ryan who developed a compact, AI-powered water-quality sensor that small farms and municipalities could install in minutes. He filed a strong U.S.

provisional, then, excited about early interest, started presenting the prototype at industry conferences and posting short demo videos online. Nine months later he filed the PCT. He thought he had plenty of time left to expand into Europe and Asia.

At month twenty-nine, when he sat down to plan national-phase entries, the bad news hit: his conference presentations and videos counted as public disclosures. Under Europe's absolute novelty rules (and in some Asian countries), the invention was now treated as no longer new. The 30-month window was also closing fast on his key markets. Ryan watched the European and Chinese territories he had targeted for his biggest revenue suddenly become unavailable forever.

The firm could not rewind time, but they salvaged what was still possible. They at once filed national-phase applications in the countries where his disclosures had not yet barred him, drafted divisional applications to handle unity-of-invention issues, and paid for premium translations in Japan and Korea. Ryan had to pivot his entire business strategy, focusing on the U.S. and the remaining open markets while strengthening the product for any second-wave opportunities. The mistake cost him two major continents and six figures in lost international revenue before he could recover.

Ryan avoided total loss because he acted the moment he learned the rules. That is the mindset I want you to adopt right now. File your first application **before** any public disclosure. Draft the PCT with every variation and alternative already included. Calendar the 30/31-month deadlines the day you file and start planning national-phase entries at least three months early. Choose your countries strategically, where your real customers and enforcement options exist, rather than trying to file everywhere. Invest in professional translations and local counsel instead of trying to save a few thousand dollars that can cost you millions later.

International protection is not about filing more patents. It is about filing smarter and earlier, so you never have to look back and wonder what you could have protected.

Key Takeaways You Can Use Today

- The 30/31-month national-phase deadline is absolute, miss it and the country is gone forever.
- Europe and most of Asia have absolute novelty: any public disclosure before filing can destroy your rights there.

- Your original PCT application must contain every detail and variation you might ever need: Europe does not allow "added subject matter."
- Translations matter more than most inventors realize; a poor one can silently narrow your claims.
- Plan jurisdictions strategically and budget for local attorneys and translations, do not file everywhere, file where it counts.
- The best international strategy starts on day one: file before you disclose, draft comprehensively, and calendar every deadline like your business depends on it, because it does.

Chapter 9: What Is a PCT Patent Application? The Global Strategy Every Serious Inventor Must Understand

If your invention even has a chance of selling beyond your home country, you need a global strategy from day one.

Products cross borders overnight. Competitors manufacture overseas. Customers search in every language. And if your patent protection stops at the U.S. border, your competitive edge stops there too. That is exactly why the Patent Cooperation Treaty (PCT) exists, and why every serious inventor who thinks bigger than one market eventually uses it.

In plain English, the PCT is an international system that lets you file one single application and preserve your right to seek patents in up to 150+ member countries. It does not give you a worldwide patent. What it gives you is something even more valuable at the early stage: time, information, and flexibility.

You file the PCT within twelve months of your first U.S. provisional or non-provisional filing (thanks to the Paris Convention). That single filing is treated as if you had filed on the same day in every member country. Then the real magic happens: an International Searching Authority (ISA) runs a global prior-art search and issues an International Search Report (ISR) plus a Written Opinion that tells you how strong your invention looks to the rest of the world. You can even request Chapter II (International Preliminary Examination) for a deeper analysis. All of this happens before you must spend the big money entering individual countries.

At the 30- or 31-month mark (counting from your earliest priority date), you decide which countries matter: Europe via the EPO, China, Japan, Korea, Canada, Australia, etc., and "enter the national phase" in each one. Only then do you pay the local filing fees, translation costs, and local attorney fees. Until that deadline you can still walk away from any country without losing a dime.

The PCT is a bridge, not the destination. It is the strategic pause that lets you evaluate the market, talk to distributors, raise capital, and get an honest preview of how your patent will fare internationally before you commit serious money.

A colleague at another patent firm told me about an inventor named Marcus who invented a rugged, solar-powered GPS tracker for commercial fishing fleets that worked even in the middle of the ocean with zero cell service. Sales in the U.S. were climbing, and he was getting serious interest from distributors in Europe, Southeast Asia, and Latin America. His first instinct was to file separate applications in every promising country right away; he was worried about copycats and did not want to lose momentum. That approach would have burned through his entire seed round in six months.

Instead, the firm filed a strong PCT application eleven months after his provisional. The International Search Report came back in four months and was surprisingly favorable. The Written Opinion gave clear guidance on how to tighten a couple of claims. Marcus used the ISR in his investor deck, which helped him close a six-figure round. At month twenty-eight they reviewed real sales data from the early international inquiries and made the smart call: enter only the European Patent Office, China, Japan, and Canada, exactly the markets where his customers and manufacturing partners were. They skipped the rest. The money he saved by not filing everywhere went straight into production tooling.

Eighteen months later the patents started issuing in the countries that mattered most. The European distributor who had been on the fence signed a multi-year deal the week the EPO patent granted. The PCT strategy ultimately saved Marcus's company from an expensive mistake and gave him the runway he needed to succeed globally.

Marcus's story is the reason I want you to see the PCT not as extra paperwork but as your global decision-making tool. It buys you up to 30 months of clarity before the big national-phase bills arrive. It gives you a worldwide search report that functions like a free early opinion on patentability. And it lets you keep every choice open while you figure out where your invention will make money.

Key Takeaways You Can Use Today

- The PCT is a single international filing that preserves your right to seek patents in 150+ countries without filing in each one at once.
- It does *not* grant a patent, it gives you a centralized search report, written opinion, and up to 30–31 months before you must enter national phase.
- You must file the PCT within 12 months of your first U.S. filing to keep priority.
- Use the ISR and optional Chapter II examination to evaluate strength and improve claims *before* spending on individual countries.

- During the national phase, you make careful choices by focusing on those markets where factors like customer demand, manufacturing opportunities, or legal enforcement are most significant.

- The PCT is the bridge that turns a U.S.-only idea into a global business asset, use it to stall, gather intelligence, and protect exactly where it counts.

Chapter 10: Why Smart Inventors Use the PCT System – The Global Patent Strategy That Saves Time, Money, and Risk

Filing globally is not the goal. Filing *strategically* is.

Most first-time inventors hear "international protection" and immediately think they must rush out and file separate patents in every country that might matter. They picture huge legal bills, stacks of translations, and local attorneys in a dozen jurisdictions, all before they even know if the product will sell. That approach burns cash and creates stress.

Smart inventors do the opposite. They use the Patent Cooperation Treaty (PCT) to file once, buy themselves up to 30 months of breathing room, get real intelligence about how strong their invention looks worldwide, and only then decide exactly which countries are worth the investment. PCT does not grant a patent, but it gives you something far more valuable at the early stage: control, flexibility, and the ability to invest based on evidence instead of hope.

The PCT was designed to solve the exact problem inventors and small companies face: you cannot afford to commit to every market on day one, yet you cannot afford to lose the rights in those markets either. With the PCT you file one international application (usually within 12 months of your first U.S. filing) and it acts as a placeholder that preserves your priority date across 150+ member countries. You get a centralized search report and written opinion that acts like an early report card on patentability. Then, at the 30- or 31-month mark, you choose, strategically, which countries to enter. The rest you simply walk away from, with no further cost.

This staged approach changes everything. You delay the big translation fees, local attorney costs, and national filing fees until you have real market data, investor interest, or sales traction. You reduce risk. You keep options open. And you look far more professional to investors, partners, and potential licensees because your PCT filing plus the search report shows you are thinking like a global business, not just a garage inventor.

A colleague at another patent firm told me about an inventor named Liam who developed a portable, battery-free water-purification device that used a simple mechanical filter and UV LED powered by a hand crank. Early sales in the U.S. were strong, and he was getting inquiries from NGOs and distributors in Africa, Southeast Asia, and Latin America. His first instinct was to file direct national applications in every promising country right away so no one could copy him. That plan would have used up his seed funding on legal and translation costs before any units shipped abroad.

The firm instead filed a strong PCT application. Four months later the International Search Report came back positive, with only a couple of minor prior-art citations that were easy to address. Liam used the report in his investor presentations and closed a funding round that let him build inventory. At month twenty-eight they reviewed real sales pipeline data and entered only the four countries that represented 80 percent of his projected international revenue: the European Patent Office (for the EU), China (for manufacturing scale), India, and South Africa. They skipped the rest. The money he saved went straight into production and distribution partnerships.

Eighteen months later the patents started granting in the countries that mattered. One of the African NGOs that had been testing prototypes signed a large-volume purchase order the week the South African patent issued. The PCT strategy ultimately saved Liam from burning through his capital on unnecessary filings and gave his company two extra years of runway.

Liam's story is the reason I want you to see the PCT as your global decision-making tool rather than extra paperwork. It lets you file once, gather intelligence, evaluate the market, raise capital, and then commit only where the opportunity is real. That is how you turn a good invention into a protected global business instead of an expensive international gamble.

Key Takeaways You Can Use Today

- The PCT lets you file once and preserve priority rights in 150+ countries, then decide later which markets are worth entering.
- You get a centralized International Search Report and Written Opinion that function as an early global patentability preview: use it to strengthen claims or pivot before spending big.
- The 30/31-month national-phase window gives you time to evaluate the market, raise money, and invest based on real data instead of hope.
- Cost deferral is the real power: delay translation and local attorney fees until you know where the customers are.
- Choose countries strategically at national phase, enter only where your market, manufacturing, or enforcement needs exist.
- Smart inventors do not file everywhere; they file intelligently. The PCT gives you the time and information to do exactly that.

Part III - Enforcement, Commercialization & Business Strategy

Chapter 11: How to Remove Copycat Products from Amazon and Walmart (Without Getting Sued Back)

You spent months. years, designing, evaluating, and launching the product you poured your heart (and savings) into. Then one morning you open Amazon and there it is: an almost identical listing, same photos, same features, half the price. Your stomach drops. The question hits instantly: Do I fight this, or do I watch my sales evaporate?

Most inventors hit "Report Infringement" within minutes. Some get lucky and the listing disappears. Others watch it come right back, and suddenly they are the ones threatened with a lawsuit. That is the part nobody talks about until it is too late.

Enforcing your rights online is powerful, but it is also a legal act with real teeth on both sides. Do it wrong and you can end up paying the copycat's legal bills instead of protecting your market.

Here is what works, and exactly how to do it without exposing yourself to a counterattack.

First, the non-negotiable: You must have an *issued* patent. A "patent pending" label, an idea, or even a filed application gives you zero leverage with Amazon or Walmart. The platforms only respond to enforceable IP rights: design patents or utility patents that have already been granted.

Second, you must monitor like a business owner, not a hobbyist. Set calendar reminders. Run your own keyword searches weekly. Copycats do not sleep; they scale fast.

Third, and this is where most people lose before they even start, you need bulletproof evidence *before* you file anything: your patent number, clean side-by-side comparisons, screenshots with dates, and a clear explanation of why the accused product infringes. Platforms do not investigate; they decide based on what you hand them.

The process itself is straightforward once you are prepared:

- On Amazon: Use Brand Registry (if you have it) or the standard Report Infringement form.
- On Walmart: Submit through their online IP complaint portal.

Be precise, professional, and ready to answer follow-up questions. If the platform removes the listing, great, but always assume the seller may file a counter-notice. That is when the real risk begins.

A colleague at another patent firm told me about an inventor named Sarah who had a clever, patented desk organizer that used a unique angled tray system to keep cables hidden and devices upright. It was selling steadily on Amazon until a seller in another state launched a near-identical version at a lower price. Sarah was furious and acted fast: she filed the takedown herself with nothing but a few screenshots and her patent number. The listing vanished overnight and she celebrated.

Three days later the counter-notice arrived. The seller claimed no infringement, accused Sarah of bad-faith interference, and threatened to sue her for lost profits and attorney fees. Amazon reinstated the listing while the dispute played out. Sarah suddenly realized she might be the one on the hook for damages, legal fees, and a potential lawsuit.

When the other firm reviewed the situation, they saw that her original complaint had been too emotional and light on evidence. They rebuilt the entire submission with cleaner diagrams, dated screenshots, a concise explanation focused on the ordinary-observer test, and a short, firm letter to the seller offering a brief window to pull the listing voluntarily. Within ten days the listing was permanently removed, the seller never followed through on the threat, and Sarah's sales rebounded.

The experience cost Sarah weeks of stress, lost sales during the dispute, and the frightening realization that a single impulsive takedown could have exposed her to significant liability. It taught her the hard way that enforcement online is a legal act with real teeth on both sides.

So, here is the practical playbook that protects you:

1. Get a professional infringement opinion *before* you click submit.

2. Keep your complaint factual, focused, and fully documented.

3. Save every screenshot, email, and platform response.

4. Understand that Amazon and Walmart are referees, not judges, if the seller pushes back hard, you may still need a cease-and-desist or litigation.

5. Treat every enforcement step as business strategy, not emotional reaction.

Chapter 12: Utility Patent Infringement – How to Know If Someone Is Stealing Your Invention (And What to Do About It)

You do not have a patent problem until the day a competitor starts making money from your exact idea.

Not something "similar." Not "inspired by." Your invention: same function, same result, same market. And suddenly every sale they make feels like it is coming straight out of your pocket.

That moment hits every patent owner eventually. The real question is not whether you *feel* infringed. It is whether you can prove it in a way that stops them or gets you paid.

Under U.S. law (35 U.S.C. § 271), infringement is straightforward on paper: if someone makes, uses, sells, offers to sell, or imports your patented invention without permission, it is infringement. No intent required. No "they knew better" needed. But here is the part that surprises most inventors: you do not enforce the invention itself. You enforce your *claims.* Every particular case rises or falls whether the competitor's product hits every element of at least one claim: literally or under the doctrine of equivalents.

That is why claim drafting is not just legal paperwork; it is the weapon that decides if you win or watch them walk away.

There are three main types to know:

- **Direct infringement**: They are doing exactly what your claim describes.
- **Induced infringement**: They are actively teaching or encouraging others to use it your way.
- **Contributory infringement**: They are supplying a key part that has no real purpose except to complete your patented invention.

Before any court decides infringement, a judge first interprets what your claims mean (the Markman hearing). That single step often decides the whole case. Then the analysis splits into literal infringement (every word match) or the doctrine of equivalents (same function, same way, same result: even if the words differ slightly, like a screw vs. a nail that does the exact same job).

Competitors know all this. They do not ignore your patent; they study the claims and design around them: removing one element, swapping in alternative technology, or exploiting a narrow claim. A weak patent does not stop them; it guides them.

If you decide to act, the remedies are powerful: lost profits or reasonable royalties, an injunction to stop them cold, and in exceptional cases (willful infringement) even their attorney fees. But enforcement is never free. Litigation can cost hundreds of thousands (sometimes millions), your patent can be challenged for invalidity, and the business fallout can affect relationships and reputation.

The smartest move is always strategy first: get a clear infringement opinion, calculate real damages, and decide your true goal: stop them completely, license and get paid, or protect your market position.

A colleague at another patent firm told me about an inventor named David who developed a specialized quick-release clamp for professional scaffolding that cut setup time in half. His utility patent had strong, carefully drafted claims covering the unique locking mechanism. Six months after launch, a competitor appeared on Amazon and at trade shows selling an almost identical clamp at a lower price. David was furious and ready to fire off a cease-and-desist letter himself.

The firm ran the exact analysis a court would use. They mapped the competitor's product against every claim element using photos, teardown videos, and product specs. The match was clear under both literal infringement and the doctrine of equivalents. They also showed David the business numbers: projected lost profits, the competitor's margins, and the realistic cost of litigation versus a licensing deal. They drafted a professional notice letter that laid out the infringement without emotion and offered a short window to negotiate a license.

Within three weeks the competitor responded. They did not want to fight; they wanted to stay in business. The confrontation was converted into a licensing agreement that gave David ongoing royalties and removed the cheap knockoff from the market. David later said the experience taught him that acting on emotion before running the claim-by-claim analysis could have turned his strongest asset into an expensive legal war.

David avoided the classic trap of acting on emotion before running the claim-by-claim analysis. That single step changed the outcome from potential loss to real profit.

Key Takeaways You Can Use Today

- You enforce your *claims*, not the invention itself, if even one claim element is missing, there may be no infringement.
- Literal infringement or doctrine of equivalents (same function, same way, same result) are the two tests that matter.

- Competitors design around weak or narrow claims, strong drafting from day one is your best defense.
- Before any letter or lawsuit, get a professional infringement analysis, calculate real damages, and define your business goal (stop them, license, or protect market share).
- Enforcement tools range from a simple cease-and-desist to full litigation, choose the one that matches your budget and objective.
- A patent is only as powerful as your willingness and ability to enforce it strategically.

Chapter 13: How to Find Investors for Your Invention (Without Losing Your Rights or Your Company)

Every inventor dreams of the moment an investor leans forward and says, "I love this idea. let us make it happen."

That moment feels like the finish line. In reality, it is the starting gun for the highest-risk phase of your journey. Because the second you open your mouth to pitch, you are disclosing your invention, negotiating ownership, and exposing the very asset you are trying to fund. Do it wrong and you can lose control of your IP, weaken your patent rights, or watch someone else walk away with the idea you spent years perfecting.

Smart inventors treat investor meetings the same way they treat patent filings: with preparation, not hope.

The first rule is simple but non-negotiable: file before you speak. A provisional patent application (or better, a non-provisional) gives you a priority date and "patent pending" status that signals seriousness. Without it, every disclosure, whether in a pitch deck, demo, or casual conversation, can start the one-year U.S. grace period clock and permanently kill your rights in Europe, China, Japan, and most of Asia, where there is no grace period at all.

Next, never disclose without a proper Non-Disclosure Agreement (NDA). A solid NDA defines what is confidential, how it can be used, and what happens if it is misused. It is your legal shield. Trade-secret protection only survives if you treat the information as secret; once you share it casually, that protection can vanish forever.

Investors are not buying your enthusiasm; they are buying reduced risk. During due diligence they will scrutinize your patent status, claim strength, prior-art exposure, and ownership clarity. A strong, issued patent or at least a well-drafted provisional tells them you have done the homework. A vague idea with no protection tells them you are a liability.

Raising money is regulated. Most early-stage deals fall under Regulation D of the Securities Act. Structure the offer correctly, disclose material facts, and work only with qualified investors, or you risk penalties, rescission demands, or even personal liability.

Ownership is the silent killer. Inventorship (who created it) is different from ownership (who controls it). Funding agreements often include assignment clauses, equity grants, or joint-development provisions. Without unambiguous language, you can end up inventing something you no longer own.

A colleague at another patent firm told me about an inventor named Tyler who had built a compact, AI-driven inventory scanner that retailers could install in minutes. Sales were growing, and a well-known angel group invited him to pitch. Excited, he sent over his pitch deck and prototypes without a signed NDA and without having filed any patent application yet. The meeting went great; the investors were enthusiastic and asked detailed technical questions. Tyler answered everything.

Two weeks later the group passed, but three months after that a similar product appeared from a company one of the investors had previously backed. Tyler's provisional filing (which he finally did after the meeting) was too late for Europe and Asia, and the claims were narrow because he had disclosed too much without protection. The investor group claimed they had developed the idea independently. Tyler had no NDA, no early filing date, and no leverage. He watched his differentiator get copied while his own international rights evaporated.

He reached out to the other firm angry and scared. They rebuilt the strategy from the ground up: filed a new continuation with broader, strategic claims, secured proper NDAs for all future meetings, and restructured his company documents so any future funding would clearly preserve his core IP ownership. Within six months he pitched a different group, this time with a strong provisional, signed NDAs, and clean ownership paperwork. The new investors not only funded him but introduced him to manufacturing partners in Asia. Tyler later said, "I almost handed my entire company to the first people who showed interest. One conversation about protection before the pitch changed the entire trajectory."

Tyler's story is the reason I want you to pause before you ever send that pitch deck. File first. Use NDAs. Structure ownership clearly. Treat every investor conversation as a business negotiation, not a trust exercise. When you do, investors see a founder who understands risk, and that is exactly what makes them want to invest.

Key Takeaways You Can Use Today

- File a patent application (provisional at minimum) *before* any investor meeting, public disclosure without protection can destroy international rights forever.

- Always use a proper NDA before sharing technical details; casual "trust me" conversations are not protection.

- Investors fund reduced risk: strong IP, clear ownership, and clean securities compliance make you far more attractive.

- Structure every funding deal so you retain control of your core invention; understand the difference between inventorship and ownership.

- Licensing can keep you in control with royalties; equity can give bigger upside but less control, choose based on your long-term vision.

- Protect first, pitch second. The investors who matter will respect the preparation, not penalize it.

Chapter 14: How to License or Sell Your Invention – What Royalties Really Look Like (And What No One Tells You)

Every inventor eventually reaches the exciting moment when someone says, "I want to take this to market for you."

That conversation feels like validation. But it is also the point where many inventors quietly give away far more than they realize or settle for far less than they could have earned. Because licensing or selling your invention is not about hope and handshakes. It is a business negotiation built on risk, value, and structure. Get the structure right and you can create long-term income that outlasts any specific product launch. Get it wrong and you can watch years of work disappear into a deal that looks good on paper but pays almost nothing.

The first decision you must make is whether you want to sell the invention outright (an assignment) or license it. Selling gives you a lump-sum payment and walks away from future upside. Licensing keeps you as the owner and lets you earn ongoing royalties, usually a percentage of net sales, while the licensee manages manufacturing, marketing, and distribution. Most inventors choose licensing because they want the long-term income stream, but the real money only shows if the deal is built correctly.

Most consumer products and hardware inventions have realistic royalty rates between 2% and 10%. Consumer goods often land at 2–5%, manufacturing tools at 2–6%, and higher-tech or biotech inventions can reach 5–15% when milestones are involved. You are not getting 25% or "half the profits." The licensee is taking the production risk, the marketing risk, the inventory risk, and the market-acceptance risk. Royalties reflect that risk split, not just the brilliance of your idea.

What moves the needle on your rate are four factors: the strength of your patent, the size of the market, the level of competition, and how far along the product already is. A strong, issued patent with broad claims gives you leverage. A weak or narrow patent makes the licensee see you as easy to design around. Large markets with real demand command higher rates. Heavy competition pushes rates down. And a product that is already selling (even in small volumes) is worth more than a napkin sketch.

The biggest negotiation points most inventors miss is the trade-off between upfront money and royalty rate. A high upfront payment (say $100,000) almost always comes with a lower royalty percentage because the licensee has already taken on more immediate risk. A low or zero upfront payment usually buys you a higher royalty rate plus milestones and minimum annual guarantees. Smart inventors use this trade-off strategically: take some cash now if you need runway but protect the long-term upside with minimum royalties (so you get paid even if sales are slow) and milestone payments (triggered by launch, sales targets, or regulatory approval).

Enforcement must be spelled out, who pays for patent defense if a copycat appears? Shared responsibility is common, but you want the licensee to have skin in the game, so they police the market.

A colleague at another patent firm told me about an inventor named Rachel who had designed a clever, space-saving collapsible drying rack for apartments that folded flat against the wall. A mid-sized home-goods manufacturer reached out after seeing her product at a trade show. They offered a simple deal: 3% royalty, no upfront payment, no minimums, and they would oversee everything. Rachel was ready to sign; she just wanted it in stores.

She brought the term sheet to the other firm first. They ran the numbers and showed her that at projected sales volume the 3% deal would net her only $18,000 in the first two years. Then they sat down with the manufacturer and negotiated: 4.5% royalty, $75,000 upfront payment, a $25,000 annual minimum royalty guarantee, and milestone payments tied to national retail launch. The manufacturer agreed because they saw the strength of her issued design and utility patents.

Two years later Rachel had already received the upfront money plus the minimum guarantees, and royalties were running well above the floor. The product is now in major retail chains, and she continues to earn every quarter. Rachel later said, "I almost traded years of income for the comfort of a quick signature. One clear breakdown of the numbers and the right structure turned that 'okay' deal into the foundation of my next product line."

Rachel avoided the classic trap of focusing only on the percentage and ignoring the full structure. That single meeting taught her, and should teach every inventor, that licensing is not a lottery. It is a business deal. File strong patents first. Understand the real royalty ranges. Negotiate upfront money, minimum guarantees, and milestones. Decide whether you want immediate cash or long-term income. And never sign until you have run the numbers and had the agreement reviewed by someone who lives in these deals every day.

When you do those things, licensing stops being a dream and starts being a predictable income stream that rewards the years you put into the invention.

Key Takeaways You Can Use Today

- Decide first: sell (lump sum, no future upside) or license (keep ownership, earn ongoing royalties).

- Realistic royalty rates for most inventions fall between 2% and 10%, higher rates come with strong patents, large markets, and low competition.

- Negotiate the trade-off: more upfront cash usually means lower royalties; lower upfront usually means higher royalties plus protections.

- Always include minimum annual royalties and milestone payments so you get paid even if the licensee moves slowly.

- Spell out enforcement responsibility: who pays to defend the patent if copycats appear.

- Run the numbers on every offer and have the agreement reviewed before you sign. Licensing rewards preparation, not hope.

Chapter 15: What Is Your Invention Really Worth? The Truth About Patent Valuation (That Most Inventors Do Not Want to Hear)

"How much is my invention worth?"

Every inventor asks this question at some point, usually right after they file the patent or right before they pitch an investor. The honest answer most do not want to hear is: "It depends… and usually it's worth less than you think."

Value is not determined by how clever, unique, or technically impressive your idea is. It is decided by three hard realities: market demand, legal strength, and commercial execution. An idea by itself has no price tag. A patent by itself has no price tag. Only an enforceable, commercially relevant patent that solves a real problem for a real market has value.

There are three standard ways patents are valued and understanding them keeps you from overestimating (or worse, underselling) what you have.

1. **Cost Approach**: What did it cost to create? This adds up R&D, prototyping, and patent filing expenses. It is the method most inventors use instinctively ("I spent $150,000, so it must be worth at least that"). The problem is obvious: the market does not reimburse effort. You can spend a fortune on something nobody wants.

2. **Market Approach**: What are comparable patents selling or licensing for? This looks at recent deals in your industry. It gives useful benchmarks, but no two inventions are identical, so it is guidance, not gospel.

3. **Income Approach**: The one that matters most. This asks: How much money will this patent generate over its life? Future licensing revenue, product sales, or cost savings are projected and then discounted for risk, because not every patent succeeds, not every market adopts, and not every product scale. Future cash is always worth less than cash today.

The single biggest driver of value is patent strength. A broad, well-drafted, issued patent that is difficult to design around can be worth millions. A narrow, weak, or easily bypassed patent is often worth close to zero, no matter how brilliant the underlying idea is. Pending applications are worth less than issued ones because they are still uncertain. Investors and buyers pay for certainty, not potential.

Market size, competition, and scalability also matter enormously. A patent that solves a $10 billion problem in a growing industry with few alternatives commands a high valuation. A patent for a tiny niche with easy workarounds does not. Early inventions with no revenue are valued on cost or comparables; commercialized inventions with proven sales are valued on actual income potential.

A colleague at another patent firm told me about an inventor named James who had developed a specialized sensor clip for commercial drones that dramatically improved flight stability in windy conditions. He had spent two years and $200,000 on development and patent filings. When he came to the firm, he was certain the patent portfolio was worth at least $2 million because "no one else has this." He wanted to license it or sell the company outright and retire early.

The firm ran a professional valuation using the income approach. They analyzed the addressable market, current drone adoption rates, competitive landscape, and the actual breadth of his claims. The patents were solid but narrower than he realized, and the total addressable market for that specific use case was far smaller than he had estimated. The realistic licensing value over the life of the patents, after discounting for risk, came in between $350,000 and $650,000 if everything went right.

James was disappointed at first. But the valuation gave him clarity instead of false hope. The firm helped him strengthen the claims with a continuation application, broadened the marketing to adjacent drone applications, and introduced him to two established drone manufacturers. Six months later he closed a licensing deal with a $150,000 upfront payment, 5% royalties, and annual minimum guarantees. The deal has already paid him more than his original cost basis and is generating ongoing income. James later said, "I was ready to walk away from a $400,000 reality because I was in love with a $2 million fantasy. One honest valuation saved me from either underselling or overvaluing my life's work."

That is the power of understanding what your invention is worth. Value is not emotional. It is strategic. It is earned through strong patents, real market demand, and disciplined execution. When you know the actual number, whether it is $50,000 or $5 million, you can make smarter decisions about licensing, selling, raising capital, or continuing to invest.

Key Takeaways You Can Use Today

- Your invention's value is not how much you spent or how clever it is: it is driven by enforceable patent strength, market size, competition, and revenue potential.

- The income approach (projected future earnings discounted for risk) is the most realistic method investors and buyers use.
- Strong, broad, issued patents command far higher valuations than weak, narrow, or pending ones.
- Inventions in their preliminary stages are assessed based on costs or similar examples, while inventions that generate revenue are valued according to actual income earned.
- Most patents have limited commercial value. The ones that create real wealth solve big problems in big markets with strong, defensible protection.
- Get an objective valuation before you pitch investors, negotiate a license, or decide to sell, knowing the real number prevents both disappointment and costly mistakes.

PART IV – RISKS & PROTECTION

Chapter 16: The Hidden Legal Risks That Can Destroy Your Company's Intellectual Property (Before You Even Go to Market)

Most companies do not fail because the product was bad. They fail because of something invisible until it is not: intellectual-property risk they never saw coming.

You pour millions into development, months into branding, and years into building momentum. Then, days before launch, or worse, weeks after, a cease-and-desist letter arrives, a lawsuit lands, or an injunction blocks your product in key markets. Suddenly the conversation shifts from growth to survival. Investors pull back, cash flow tightens, and the entire company is forced into damage-control mode.

This is not rare. It is the quiet pattern I see repeatedly with founders and CEOs who treated IP as a "legal detail" instead of a core business risk. The threats are not always obvious, but once they surface, they are immediate, expensive, and often irreversible.

The biggest hidden risk is patent infringement. Under U.S. law you can infringe without ever copying intentionally or even knowing the patent existed. If your product practices even one claim of an active patent, you are exposed to federal litigation, potential triple damages for willful infringement, attorney fees, and, most damaging, an injunction that can take your product off the market entirely.

That is why every smart launch begins with a Freedom-to-Operate (FTO) analysis. It is the due diligence step most companies skip because "we'll deal with it if it comes up." When it comes up, redesigns become rushed and expensive, settlements turn punitive, and investor confidence evaporates.

International risks are even more unforgiving. Disclose your invention publicly before filing and you can permanently lose patent rights in Europe and most of Asia, where absolute novelty rules apply. Miss the 30/31-month national-phase deadline after filing a PCT application and entire countries are closed to you forever. A weak or poorly drafted patent portfolio creates a false sense of security that competitors quickly exploit.

Contractual and business-tort risks add another layer. An over-aggressive enforcement letter can trigger claims of tortious interference or unfair competition. Poorly structured development agreements can create joint-ownership disputes or unintended assignments of your IP.

A colleague at another patent firm told me about a CEO named Michael who was the founder of a fast-growing med-tech startup with a breakthrough wearable monitor for chronic respiratory patients. The product was elegant, the clinical data was strong, and a major distributor was ready to launch in the U.S. and Europe. Michael had a provisional patent and assumed that was enough. He skipped the full Freedom-to-Operate search to save time and money, pushed the product into beta testing, and began public demos at trade shows.

Three weeks before the official launch, a competitor sent a detailed cease-and-desist letter claiming infringement on two issued patents. The competitor had performed its own FTO years earlier and was ready to sue for willful infringement. Because Michael had publicly disclosed features before filing the non-provisional, his European rights were already lost. The distributor immediately paused the rollout. Investors who had been circling for a Series B round went silent.

Michael called the other firm the same day the letter arrived. They conducted an expedited FTO that identified design-around options, filed a strengthened continuation application, and negotiated a licensing deal that turned the threat into a paid partnership. The product launched on time in the U.S., the European market was salvaged through a different filing strategy, and the company closed its Series B at a higher valuation than originally projected. Michael later told his team, "I almost bet the entire company on the assumption that 'no one will notice.' One missed FTO analysis nearly ended everything we had built."

Michael's story is the reason every CEO should treat intellectual property risk the same way they treat financial or regulatory risk: proactively, not reactively. The fix is straightforward once you decide to face it.

1. Run a professional Freedom-to-Operate analysis before you finalize the product design.

2. File strong, strategic patents early, before any public disclosure.

3. Build and maintain a global patent portfolio with the 30/31-month PCT deadlines locked in your calendar.

4. Integrate IP into every major business decision: launches, fundraising, partnerships, and M&A.

5. Structure every contract and development agreement to protect ownership and limit expanded liability.

IP risk is invisible until the moment it is not. By then the cost is no longer just legal fees, it has lost market share, damaged investor confidence, and sometimes the company itself. Companies that win are not just innovative. They are the ones that protect what they cannot afford to lose.

Key Takeaways You Can Use Today

- Patent infringement can happen unintentionally, run a Freedom-to-Operate analysis before launch, not after a lawsuit arrives.
- Public disclosure before filing can permanently destroy rights in Europe and Asia: file first, talk later.
- Weak or narrow patents create false security; invest in strong, broad claims that are difficult to design around.
- Missed PCT national-phase deadlines are irreversible, calendar them the day you file.
- IP risk affects valuation, fundraising, and M&A, treat it as a core business issue, not a legal afterthought.
- Proactive IP strategy prevents crises; reactive strategy pays for them.

Chapter 17: The Patent Strategy CEOs Get Wrong – Why Filing a Patent Is Not Enough to Protect Your Market

Most companies do not lose their competitive edge because they forgot to file a patent. They lose it because they thought filing *one* patent was enough.

They invest years and millions in R&D, celebrate when the patent issues, and then watch a competitor launch an identical product that simply "designs around" their claims. Suddenly the patent that felt like armor becomes little more than an expensive piece of paper hanging on the wall.

The hard truth every CEO needs to hear is this: your patent does not protect your idea; your claims protect your business. Filing is the beginning of protection, not the end. What separates the companies that dominate their market from the ones that get copied is strategy: broad, well-drafted claims, full supporting disclosure, and a deliberate portfolio built with continuations, divisionals, and international filings.

Too many CEOs treat patents like a checkbox: "We filed, we're protected." They accept narrow claims to get the patent issued faster, skip continuations because they seem like extra work, and never build the layered portfolio that blocks competitors. The result is predictable: competitors study the claims, tweak one element, and walk right past the patent.

A colleague at another patent firm told me about a CEO named David who was leading a rapidly scaling industrial IoT company. His team had developed a breakthrough sensor array that cut predictive-maintenance downtime by 40 percent. They filed a single utility patent with what they thought were strong claims, raised a Series B on the strength of the "patented technology," and launched to great fanfare. Six months later a competitor released an almost identical system that simply swapped one connector type and changed the mounting angle. Sales stalled. The competitor's product was cheaper, and David's patent attorney told him the claims were too narrow to enforce.

David reached out in frustration. The firm showed him the gap. The original patent had solid but limited claims, no continuation strategy, and no international filings beyond the U.S. They immediately filed three continuation applications to broaden the core claims, added new diagnostic algorithms, and filed a PCT to secure key European and Asian markets before the 30-month window closed. Within fourteen months the new patents issued with significantly broader protection. The competitor, seeing the strengthened portfolio, redesigned again into something uniquely different.

David's sales recovered, the company closed a larger Series C, and he now treats the patent portfolio as a living asset reviewed in every quarterly board meeting.

David later said, "I thought filing the patent meant we were done. It was just the first move. Building the full strategy is what protected the company."

That is the shift I want every CEO to make. Stop thinking of patents as isolated filings and start treating them as a strategic system. Demand broad, strategic claims supported by comprehensive disclosure. Use continuations and divisionals to evolve the portfolio as the product improves. File internationally through PCT before deadlines expire. Build a fortress, not a single wall.

When you do, your patents stop being a cost center and become the moat that keeps competitors out and investors in.

Key Takeaways You Can Use Today

- Your patent does not protect your idea; your *claims* define what you own. Narrow or poorly drafted claims are easy for competitors to design around.

- Filing once is not a strategy. Build a living portfolio with continuations, continuation-in-part (CIP), and divisionals to adapt and expand protection as the invention evolves.

- Strong patents require broad yet defensible claims, full disclosure of variations and alternatives, and awareness of prior art, weak patents create false security.

- International protection must be planned from day one. Use the PCT and never miss the 30/31-month national-phase deadlines.

- Treat patents as a core business system, not a legal checkbox. Companies that win do not just file patents, they build strategies competitors cannot break.

- If you don't control your IP, you don't control your market.

Chapter 18: Your Company's Most Undervalued Asset – How Intellectual Property Drives Market Control and Company Valuation

Most CEOs can tell you their revenue run rate, their gross margin, and the size of their TAM. Ask them what their company is truly worth and they will point to the product, the team, or the latest funding round.

They rarely point to the one asset that determines long-term dominance: intellectual property.

IP is not a legal line item. It is the strategic moat that lets you exclude competitors, command premium pricing, license revenue streams, and dramatically increase enterprise value. When investors, acquirers, or partners look at your company, one of the first questions is always some version of "What do you own that others cannot replicate?" Strong IP answers that question with clarity and power. Weak or missing IP answers it with silence.

From a CEO perspective, intellectual property is the right to exclude others from making, using, selling, or importing what you invented. Utility patents protect function, design patents protect appearance, trademarks protect brand, and trade secrets protect everything you keep confidential. Together they create layered protection around the very things that make your company different.

This is not theoretical. Companies with strong, strategically built IP portfolios consistently command higher valuations, close better licensing deals, and survive competitive attacks that destroy companies without protection. They do not just compete with price or features; they control the market.

A colleague at another patent firm told me about a CEO named Sarah who was leading a fast-growing SaaS platform that used proprietary algorithms to predict equipment failure in manufacturing plants. The technology was excellent, adoption was accelerating, and she had just received a term sheet from a top-tier VC firm at a $45 million pre-money valuation. During due diligence, the investors asked one question she was unprepared for: "Walk us through your IP moat." Sarah had filed a single provisional patent and assumed that was enough. The technical advisor for the investors promptly noticed that the claims were limited, lacked international coverage, and that important algorithms were still being managed as trade secrets without adequate NDAs. The valuation dropped to $28 million and the term sheet was rewritten with heavier protective covenants.

Sarah called the other firm the same afternoon. They filed three continuation applications to broaden the core claims, added design patents on the unique dashboard interface, secured international PCT filings before the deadlines closed, and implemented a comprehensive trade-secret protection program. Six weeks later they presented the strengthened portfolio back to investors. The deal closed at the original $45 million valuation plus an extra $5 million because the new IP made the company far more defensible. Two years later the company was acquired at a valuation more than triple the original round, largely because the buyer paid a premium for the now-impenetrable IP fortress.

Sarah later told her board, "I thought IP was a legal checkbox. The investors taught me it is the single biggest driver of what our company is worth. One strategic portfolio turned a discounted deal into the foundation for our exit."

That is the shift every CEO needs to make. Stop treating patents and IP as a cost center or a legal afterthought. Start treating them as the strategic asset they are. File early and often. Build a portfolio, not a single filing. Use continuations to evolve protection as the product improves. Secure international rights before you disclose. And integrate IP into every major business conversation, fundraising, M&A, licensing, and competitive strategy.

When you do, intellectual property stops being the most undervalued asset on your balance sheet and becomes the one that determines how much your company is worth, and how long it will stay that way.

Key Takeaways You Can Use Today

- Intellectual property is your company's most undervalued asset because it is the only thing that legally excludes others from copying what makes you different.

- Strong IP drives higher valuations, better licensing revenue, pricing power, and investor confidence; weak or missing IP does the opposite.

- Investors and acquirers evaluate patent strength, claim breadth, enforceability, and global coverage, treat IP as a core business metric, not a legal side note.

- Build a living portfolio with continuations, divisionals, and international filings rather than relying on a single patent.

- The companies that dominate their markets do not just innovate; they own what they innovate. Make IP strategy a board-level priority, not an afterthought.

Chapter 19: Beware Of Invention Promotion Companies – The Scams That Cost Inventors Millions (And How To Spot Them Before They Spot You)

Every inventor dreams of the day someone says, "We'll oversee everything: patenting, marketing, licensing, the works."

That phone call or slick website ad feels like the break you've been waiting for. But for far too many inventors, it becomes the most expensive mistake of their career.

Invention promotion companies (also called invention submission or marketing firms) promise to turn your idea into a profitable product. They charge thousands, sometimes tens of thousands, of dollars upfront for "evaluations," patent searches, prototype development, and marketing packages. The FTC and USPTO have issued warnings regarding these companies for decades, as most fail to provide significant value or results.

The Federal Trade Commission has shut down multiple operations that bilked consumers out of millions. The pattern is always the same: high-pressure sales, glowing success stories that are exaggerated or are fake, and "positive" evaluations that are never negative. The USPTO maintains a public list of complaints against these firms and requires them to disclose specific information before signing a contract, including how many inventions they've evaluated in the past five years and how many resulted in commercial success (the real number is usually tiny).

The truth most inventors never hear until it's too late: legitimate help exists, but it almost never starts with a company promising to do everything for a big upfront fee. Real protection and commercialization come from working with licensed patent attorneys or agents, filing your own provisional application when ready, and focusing on strong claims, not paying someone to "shop" your idea.

Here's how that promise turned into a nightmare for an inventor who almost lost his shot at real protection.

Alex had invented a simple, low-cost attachment that turned any standard bicycle into an e-bike in minutes. Excited after seeing an online ad, he contacted a firm that promised a full patent package, market research, and licensing introductions for $12,500. They sent glowing "success stories," rushed him to sign, and collected the fee within days. The "patent search" came back positive, they filed a provisional, and then… radio silence. Months later Alex learned the provisional was poorly drafted, the marketing never happened, and the firm had been the subject of multiple FTC complaints. He had spent his entire development budget and now faced a weak filing that left him exposed internationally.

When he finally reached our office, the damage was partially reversible. We filed proper continuation applications, strengthened the claims, and helped him move forward with legitimate licensing outreach. But the $12,500 and months of delay were gone forever. Alex later told me, "I thought I was paying for experts. I was really paying for a lesson in what not to do. One quick check of the FTC and USPTO sites would have saved me everything."

That is the lesson I want every inventor to take away. Invention promotion companies are not illegal, but many operate in the gray area of deception. The FTC's consumer advice is clear: honest firms are rare, and dishonest ones lie about profit potential to collect upfront fees for services you can often do better yourself or with a qualified attorney.

How to Protect Yourself (Red Flags and Smart Moves)

- **Check official sources first**: Search the USPTO's public complaint list for the company and review the FTC's invention marketing scam page.
- **Demand required disclosures**: Federal law requires promoters to tell you in writing how many inventions they've evaluated, how many received positive evaluations, and how many made money for clients.
- **Never pay large upfront fees for marketing or licensing help**: Legitimate commercialization usually comes after you have strong IP, not before.
- **Work only with registered patent attorneys or agents**: Check the USPTO's roster of practitioners.
- **File your own provisional first**: It costs far less and gives you real protection while you evaluate options.
- **If it sounds too good to be true, it is**: "Guaranteed success," "We'll make you rich," or pressure to act fast are classic scam signals.

Key Takeaways You Can Use Today

- Invention promotion companies often charge thousands for services that deliver little or nothing: FTC and USPTO warnings have been consistent for decades.

- Always check the USPTO complaint list and FTC resources before signing anything.
- Demand the legally required written disclosures about the company's record.
- File your own provisional patent application first for real protection at a fraction of the cost.
- Work only with licensed patent attorneys or agents, never pay large upfront marketing fees to promoters.
- If it sounds too good to be true (guaranteed success, huge royalties, rush you to pay), walk away.

Chapter 20: Common Scams Perpetrated on Inventors After a Patent Application Has Been Filed – The 10 Traps That Cost Inventors Millions (And how the FTC, USPTO, and Courts Expose Them)

You have finally filed your patent application. You have "patent pending" status. You sense that you have made a significant move and are now safeguarded.

That is exactly when the scammers strike hardest.

Once your application is public record, your name, address, and invention details become easy targets. Sophisticated fraudsters mine USPTO databases daily and flood inventors with "official-looking" offers, urgent demands, and "exclusive opportunities." The FTC, USPTO, and federal/state court records show the same ten frauds repeated year after year, costing inventors tens of thousands of dollars each and sometimes destroying their ability to protect the invention they just filed.

Here are the ten most common post-filing frauds, documented directly from FTC enforcement actions, USPTO public complaint lists, and court cases:

1. **Fake USPTO Maintenance-Fee or Renewal Notices** Scammers send letters or emails that look like official USPTO documents demanding immediate payment for "maintenance fees," "renewal," or "official registration" services that do not exist. The USPTO never solicits payments this way. (FTC consumer alerts and USPTO scam-prevention pages document this exact tactic.)

2. **"Patent Marketing" or "Licensing Brokerage" Packages** Companies contact you offering to "shop" your now-pending patent to manufacturers for a large upfront fee ($8,000–$65,000+). They promise royalties and success stories but deliver little or nothing. See FTC v. World Patent Marketing (2017–2018), where the FTC recovered millions for consumers after similar schemes.

3. **"International Patent Filing" or "Global Protection" Scams** Firms claim they will file your patent in Europe, China, Japan, etc., for an extra fee. They take the money but never file—or file worthless documents. USPTO and FTC warnings list this as one of the most frequent post-PCT frauds.

4. **"Patent Award" or "Invention Registry" Plaque/Certificate Schemes** You receive offers for "official" plaques, wall certificates, or

inclusion in private "inventor registries" for $200–$2,000. These have zero legal value. USPTO scam-prevention materials explicitly list these as worthless solicitations.

5. **Phishing Emails and Texts Impersonating USPTO Examiners** Scammers spoof USPTO phone numbers or email addresses, reference your specific application number, and demand immediate payment or personal information "to avoid abandonment." FTC alerts (2025) and USPTO spoofing warnings document the surge in these targeted attacks after filing.

6. **"Patent Enforcement" or "Litigation Funding" Offers** Firms promise to sue infringers on your behalf or provide "free" litigation funding in exchange for a huge percentage of any recovery, usually requiring upfront fees. Few fulfill their promises; most vanish after being paid. Court records from FTC actions show repeated patterns of these empty promises.

7. **Fake "Continuation" or "Patent Strengthening" Services** Unregistered entities offer to file continuations or amendments for you at a premium. They botch the filings, miss deadlines, or simply take the fee and vanish, leaving your application vulnerable.

8. **"Accelerated Approval" or "Special USPTO Relationship" Packages** Scammers claim they have "inside connections" to speed up examination or guarantee issuance for an extra fee. The USPTO has no preferred services. Multiple FTC and USPTO alerts flag this as a classic post-filing hook.

9. **"Product Development" and "Manufacturing Introduction" Scams** After filing, promoters offer to build prototypes, connect you with manufacturers, or handle "turnkey" production for large upfront payments. They deliver nothing or low-quality work, then disappear. FTC "Project Mousetrap" cases and ongoing complaints show this remains common.

10. **"Royalty Guarantee" or "Success Story" Add-On Packages** Companies circle back after filing with "enhanced marketing" packages that guarantee royalties or media exposure for another large fee. They use the fact that your application is now public to pressure you. FTC settlements repeatedly cite fabricated success stories as the core deception.

A colleague at another patent firm told me about an inventor who had just received a notice of allowance on his utility patent and was immediately contacted by a "patent marketing" firm offering a "guaranteed licensing program" for $9,995. The firm promised introductions to major manufacturers and a "success fee" only if a deal closed. The inventor paid. The firm sent a generic list of companies and never followed through. When the inventor tried to get his money back, the contract's fine print made it almost impossible. The FTC later investigated the firm for deceptive practices, but by then the inventor had lost both the money and critical time he could have used to negotiate real deals himself.

That is one of the ten common post-filing traps that continue to cost inventors millions every year.

Key Takeaways You Can Use Today

- After filing, your application becomes public, scammers use that data to target you with urgent, official-looking offers.
- Always verify any solicitation against official FTC and USPTO resources before paying a dime.
- Never pay large upfront fees for marketing, licensing, enforcement, or "accelerated" services from unsolicited companies.
- The USPTO maintains a public complaint list specifically for invention promoters, check it.
- Legitimate help comes from registered patent attorneys, not promoters promising guarantees or success stories.
- If it references your specific application number and demands immediate payment or sounds too good to be true, it almost certainly is a scam.

CONCLUSION

You have reached the end of this book, but the real work, and the real opportunity, starts now.

You now know what most inventors never learn until it is too late: patents are not just legal paperwork. They are strategic business weapons. Design patents protect the way your product looks. Utility patents protect the way it works. Provisional applications buy you time. PCT filings open the world. Strong claims, smart portfolios, and proactive enforcement are what separate the inventors who get copied from the ones who control their market.

You also know the hidden dangers: the 20% myth, the invention-promotion frauds, the missed international deadlines, the weak filings that look official but offer no real protection, and the post-filing traps that target you the moment your application becomes public.

I wrote this book because I have sat across from too many brilliant, hardworking inventors who lost years of effort and life savings: not because their idea was bad, but because no one ever gave them the straight talk in plain English before the damage was done. I have seen the quiet devastation when a single preventable mistake destroys an inventor's dream. I never want that to happen to you.

You now hold the complete playbook. You know how to file the right way, enforce the right way, license or sell the right way, value your invention realistically, and protect yourself from the people who prey on hope.

The next step is yours.

Act. File early. Build a strong portfolio. Run your Freedom-to-Operate search. Use NDAs. Structure every deal intelligently. And treat your intellectual property as the most valuable asset your company will ever own.

If you don't control your IP, you don't control your future.

Your idea deserves more than hope. It deserves a real strategy.

Protect it fiercely. Commercialize it wisely. And build the future you envisioned.

You have this.

Ruben Alcoba, Esq.

Registered Patent Attorney

Alcoba Law Group, P.A.

BACK MATTER

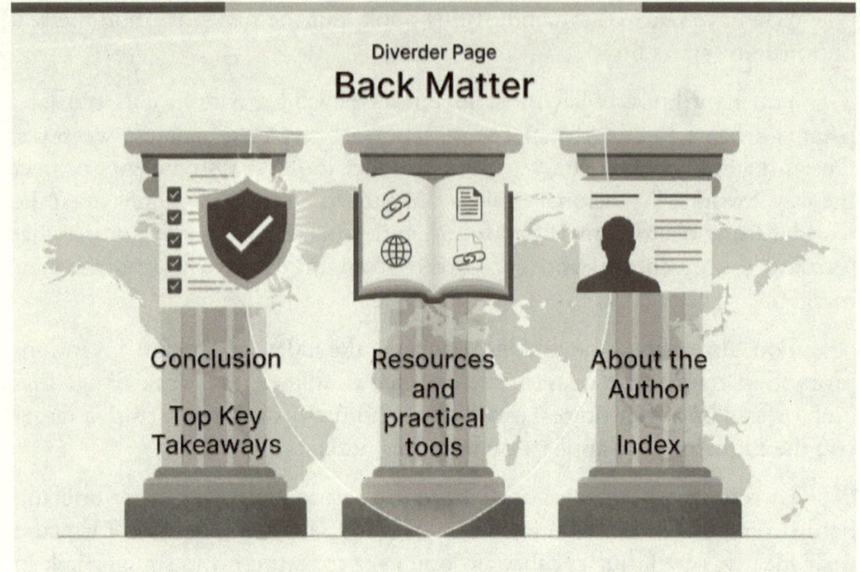
Diverder Page
Back Matter
Conclusion
Top Key Takeaways
Resources and practical tools
About the Author
Index

TOP 20 KEY TAKEAWAYS FROM THE BOOK

1. There is **no 20% rule** in design patent law, only the ordinary observer test matters.

2. Design patents protect only what is shown in the drawings: file multiple variations for real protection.

3. You **cannot** file a provisional application for a design patent, file the full non-provisional application from day one.

4. A U.S. provisional can destroy your international rights if you disclose publicly or miss the 30/31-month deadline.

5. The PCT system is the smartest way to file globally: one application, centralized search, and time to decide where to enter.

6. Utility patents protect function; design patents protect appearance; most products need both.

7. Filing a patent is not enough, **claims** define what you own, and weak claims get designed around.

8. Build a living patent portfolio with continuations, CIPs, and divisionals instead of a single filing.

9. Run a Freedom-to-Operate (FTO) analysis **before** launch to avoid infringement lawsuits.

10. Public disclosure before filing can permanently kill your rights in Europe and Asia.

11. Realistic royalty rates for most inventions are 2–10%; negotiate upfront payments, minimum guarantees, and milestones.

12. Investors and buyers value **enforceable IP** more than the idea itself, strong patents raise valuation.

13. Invention promotion companies often charge large upfront fees for little or no results, check the USPTO complaint list and FTC warnings first.

14. After filing, scammers target you with fake maintenance notices, marketing packages, and enforcement schemes: verify everything against official sources.

15. Treat IP as a core business asset, not a legal checkbox, integrate it into fundraising, launches, and strategy.

16. Licensing keeps you in control with ongoing royalties; selling gives immediate cash but no future upside.

17. Patent strength, market size, and enforceability determine what your invention is truly worth, get an objective valuation.

18. International strategy must start on day one, use the PCT and never miss national-phase deadlines.

19. Strong claims + proactive enforcement = market control; weak claims = false security.

20. The companies (and inventors) that win are not the ones who file the most patent, they are the ones who file the smartest and protect what they cannot afford to lose.

RESOURCES FOR INVENTORS

- USPTO Official Website: www.uspto.gov
- USPTO Scam Prevention & Published Complaints: www.uspto.gov/patents/basics/using-legal-services/scam-prevention
- FTC Consumer Advice on Invention Marketing Scams: consumer.ftc.gov/articles/invention-marketing-scams
- USPTO Patent Search: patft.uspto.gov
- Registered Patent Attorneys/Agents Roster: www.uspto.gov/learning-and-resources/patent-and-trademark-practitioners/roster-active
- FTC Report Fraud: reportfraud.ftc.gov

LEGAL DISCLAIMER

This book is for general informational and educational purposes only. It does not constitute legal advice and does not create an attorney-client relationship. Always consult a registered patent attorney licensed in your area before taking any action regarding your invention or intellectual property.

ABOUT THE AUTHOR

Ruben Alcoba, Esq. is the founder and managing attorney of Alcoba Law Group, P.A., a boutique intellectual property law firm based in Miami, Florida. As a registered patent attorney with the United States Patent and Trademark Office (Registration No. 44,499) and a member of the Florida Bar, Ruben has personally managed more than 2,500 patent and trademark matters over the past 26 years.

His practice focuses on helping inventors, entrepreneurs, and growing companies secure, protect, and monetize their intellectual property through strategic patent and trademark prosecution, licensing, enforcement, and global IP planning. Ruben is known for translating complex patent law into clear, actionable advice that business owners and inventors can use, whether they are filing their first provisional application or building a multi-country portfolio to support a national launch.

Ruben's clients range from independent inventors and startups to established businesses expanding into the United States. He has guided clients through every stage of the IP lifecycle: from the first drawing on a napkin to successful licensing deals and exits.

When he is not practicing law, Ruben is passionate about empowering the next generation of creators to avoid the costly mistakes he has seen too many times. This book is the culmination of that mission: to put practical, battle-tested IP knowledge directly into the hands of the inventors and CEOs who need it most.

You can learn more at www.miamipatents.com.

WORK WITH RUBEN ALCOBA, ESQ.

If you are serious about protecting your invention or business, you should not be guessing your way through the patent system.

At **Alcoba Law Group, P.A.**, we help inventors and companies:

- Develop patent strategies that create real protection
- Avoid costly legal mistakes
- Turn intellectual property into business assets

Schedule a Consultation:

alcoba@alcobalaw.com
305-362-8118

www.ingramcontent.com/pod-product-compliance
Lightning Source LLC
LaVergne TN
LVHW090536110826
845146LV00003B/1125

* 9 7 9 8 9 9 4 5 8 7 2 1 8 *